EXPLORING ENERGY

ENERGY FROM THE SUN

JAN BURGESS

Editorial planning
Deborah Tyler

 SCHOOLHOUSE PRESS

Photographic credits

t = top b = bottom l = left r = right

cover: ZEFA, The Hutchison Library

5 Camilla Jessel; 7, 9, 10, 13 Science Photo Library;
14 ZEFA; 20 Andrew Mounter/Seaphot; 22 ZEFA;
23 South American Pictures; 26 Michael Holford;
27 South American Pictures; 28 ZEFA; 30 The
Hutchison Library; 31*t* Alex Williams/Seaphot;
31*b* Geoscience Features Picture Library; 32*t* ZEFA;
32*b* South American Pictures; 34, 35 ZEFA; 36 The
Hutchison Library; 37*t* ZEFA; 37*b*, 38 Science Photo
Library; 39*t* ZEFA; 39*b* IT Power Limited; 43*t*, 43*b*
Science Photo Library; 44 Leroy Granmis/Seaphot;
45 ZEFA

Note to the reader
In this book there are some words in the text which are printed in **bold** type. This shows that the
word is listed in the glossary on page 46. The glossary gives a brief explanation of words which may
be new to you.

Contents

Introduction

The sun shines on the earth every day. It pours down light and warmth in a way that we take for granted. Think what it would be like without the sun. In a cold, dark world, plants could not grow. If there were no plants, there would be no food for animals. If there were no plants and animals, people could not survive.

The sun makes things grow. The sun gives us food and warmth. It also has **energy** stored in every ray. We cannot see or touch this energy, but we can use it. In science, the word "energy" means "something that can do work."

Kinds of Energy

There are different kinds of energy. On a windy day, you can watch sailboats move across the water. They are blown by the energy of the wind.

A still pool of water does not look as though it has much energy. However, if that water runs out of the pool into a stream, it can turn a waterwheel to grind flour. The water gains energy as it flows along. The energy of movement is called **kinetic energy**.

After you have run a race, you will feel tired because you have used up a lot of energy. Everything you do needs energy. Even sleeping takes up some energy, though not as much as running. We get new energy from the food we eat. Food is the **fuel** which makes our bodies go.

Machines help us to do work. A machine can dig up a road far more quickly than a person using a shovel.

Uses of energy throughout the world

coal

oil

natural gas

wood and plants

other sources of energy e.g. nuclear energy

sun

wind

water

water

earth's heat

Machines also need fuel to make them go. They use oil in the form of gasoline or diesel. When this fuel is burned in the engine, it releases energy and makes the machine work.

Stored Energy

We cannot make energy, but we can store it until we need it. We store food in our bodies to make our muscles work when we need them to do something. The animals and plants in the food we eat used energy from the sun to grow. They are a store of the sun's energy.

▲ Running around playing a game uses up a lot of energy. Sunbathing or sitting reading a book takes up less energy.

Today, we often use coal and oil to make machines work. Coal and oil are made of tiny plants and animals which lived millions of years ago. Coal and oil are called **fossil fuels**. Those tiny plants and animals used the sun's energy to grow. You can think of fossil fuels as stores of the sun's energy which shone down on the earth millions of years ago.

The Birth of the Sun

1. Stars are born in clouds of dust and gas.
2. The dust and gas are pulled together.
3. The shrinking clouds get hotter.
4. Energy streams to the surface as the center of the cloud gets hotter.
5. The star begins its life by giving off heat and light.
6. Billions of years later, the star has used up most of its energy. It glows red. The gases trapped inside make it swell up to become a star called a red giant.
7. The outer layers of the star begin to drift away. A smaller heavy core is left behind. This is called a white dwarf star.
8. The star gets cooler and dimmer.
9. This black dwarf star has no energy left.

6

Ever since people first lived on the earth, they have looked up into the sky. They have wondered what was out there and how it all began.

Today, most scientists believe that more than ten billion years ago, there was an explosion, or the **big bang**. The material thrown out by the explosion whirled outwards through space.

Deep in space, clouds of dust and gas gathered together. Some clouds became thicker. The clouds heated up to such high temperatures that they started to glow and give off light. This was how the **stars** were born, and one of them was our sun. Groups of millions of stars, or **galaxies**, were formed. There are countless galaxies in space. Together, they make up the **universe**.

Our Galaxy

Because the universe is so big, it is difficult to imagine that most of the stars we can see in the sky are part of just one galaxy. This is our own galaxy, which we call the Milky Way. The Milky Way contains millions and millions of stars. On a clear night, it is possible to see the Milky Way. It looks like a narrow band of stars. This is because it is shaped like a plate and we are looking at it from the side.

All the time, new stars are being born and old ones are dying. Stars shine most brightly when they are young. Gradually, they cool down. At the end of their lives, stars cool off until they contain no more heat or light. Then they are dead.

Around the Sun

Our part of the Milky Way is called the **solar system**. It was formed about 4.6 billion years ago, and it is found at the edge of the Milky Way.

In the solar system, there are nine **planets**, many other smaller bodies, and the sun. The planets move around the sun and follow set courses, or **orbits**. Unlike stars, planets do not glow with heat and light. The planets look as if they are shining if you see them in the night sky. This is because they are acting like a mirror and are **reflecting** the sun's light.

◄ Our sun is now a middle-aged star. Scientists believe it will go on shining for another five billion years. The sun will gradually burn off its gases. It will cool and lose its energy.

► This is the Andromeda galaxy. It is one of the closest galaxies to us. You can see it showing up like a hazy patch in the night sky. Its size and shape looks a little like our own galaxy.

The Sun and the Earth

▼ Mercury is the closest planet to the sun. It is about 36 million miles away. On the side facing the sun, the temperature is hot enough to melt tin or lead. Pluto is right on the edge of the solar system, about 3.7 billion miles away from the sun. Scientists believe it may be made of frozen gases.

Distances in space are so great that it is hard to imagine them. For example, the earth is more than 93 million miles away from the sun, which is our nearest star.

To stop the numbers from getting too big to work with, scientists often measure distances in space in **light-years**. A light-year is how far a ray of light can travel in a year, which is 5.9 trillion miles. Our solar system is 30,000 light-years away from the center of our galaxy. Sunlight takes eight minutes to reach the earth.

The Sun's Pull

The sun is 864,000 miles across, which is more than a hundred times wider than the earth. If you think of the sun as a soccer ball, the earth would be the size of a pea some thirty-three yards away.

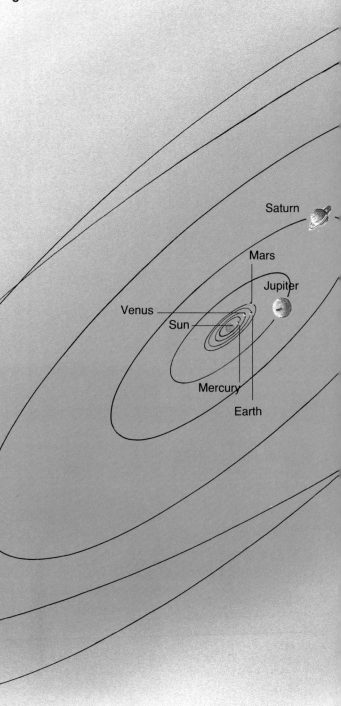

Saturn

Mars

Jupiter

Venus

Sun

Mercury

Earth

Pluto

Neptune

Uranus

Day and Night

As well as traveling around the sun, the earth also spins. It turns right around once every twenty-four hours. This means that each part of the earth has a regular pattern of day and night. If you could go out into space and look down on the earth, you would see that the half of the earth facing the sun is in sunlight. There it is day. The other half is in darkness and there it is night. As the earth spins around, it looks as though the sun is moving across the sky. In fact, it is not the sun which is moving, but our earth.

The earth and all the planets move in fixed orbits around the sun. This is because the sun is larger than all the objects around it. As it spins, it makes a pulling force called **gravity**. Gravity holds the planets in the solar system. The earth is smaller than the sun. Therefore, its gravity is not as strong. However, the moon circles around the earth, and is held in place by the earth's gravity.

▶ This picture was taken during an eclipse, when the moon comes between the sun and the earth. Then, we can see that the sun is not a solid ball. It is circled by hot gases. These hot gases are just one sign of the sun's energy.

Inside the Sun

Scientists cannot see inside the sun, but by using special instruments, they can see what is going on at the surface. They can measure how much heat and light is given off, and figure out what is happening inside.

A Ball of Fire

For many years, scientists thought that the sun was a ball of burning rock. In fact, it is made of two gases, **hydrogen** and **helium**. The sun gives off a tremendous amount of heat. Its nearest planet, Mercury, is scorched by the sun. On the side facing the sun, Mercury reaches 752°F. It would be far too hot for any form of life to survive.

Parts of the Sun

The sun's gases are hottest and most dense right in the center, or **core**. There, the temperature is about 35 million °F. This is where the sun's heat and light energy come from.

Energy moves outward from the core. The energy then moves to the next part of the sun as rays. This is called the **radiative zone**. Then, the rays move even farther out to an area filled with gases. This part of the sun becomes so hot that the gases begin to boil and roll over like milk heating up in a pot. This is called the **convective zone**.

At last, the sun's energy reaches the surface, or **photosphere**. Light and heat from the photosphere pour out into space.

All around the sun are the gases of the sun's atmosphere. This is called the **chromosphere**. Farther out still is the **corona**. The corona contains thin, hot gas which spreads out for millions of miles into space.

◀ The sun looks like an orange from far away. The marks are storms on the sun's surface.

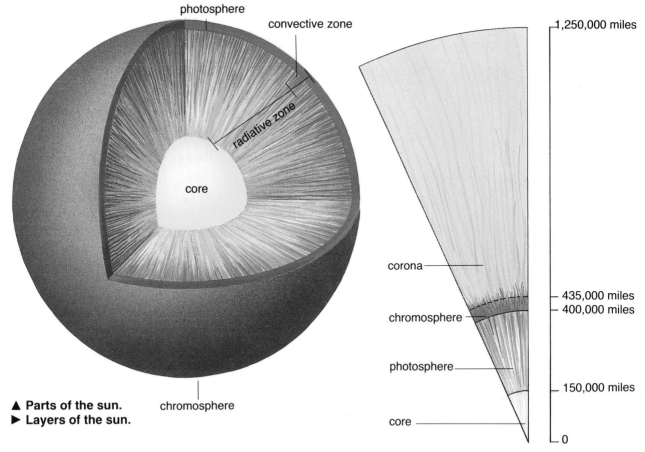

photosphere

convective zone

radiative zone

core

1,250,000 miles

corona

chromosphere

photosphere

core

435,000 miles
400,000 miles

150,000 miles

0

▲ **Parts of the sun.**
▶ **Layers of the sun.**

chromosphere

The Stormy Sun

The surface of the sun is not smooth. Powerful telescopes show that it is speckled all over. This is because streams of gas rise and fall in the convective zone beneath.

Dark patches, or sunspots, show up on the sun's surface. After a few days or weeks, they fade away again. Sunspots look dark because they are cooler than the rest of the sun's surface. Sunspots are only about 7,200°F compared with 9,900°F elsewhere.

Scientists can tell how fast the sun is turning. They watch the sunspots and see how soon they come back to the same position again. The sun turns once in twenty-five days. However, the earth is also moving around the sun, so we see a spot come back after twenty-seven days.

Fierce storms also take place on the surface of the sun, especially when a lot of sunspots appear. In a sun storm, giant **flares** of gas leap out into space. The flares have been made by an explosion beneath the sun's surface. These send out a stream of matter which travels through space. When it reaches the earth, lights of different colors make patterns in the sky at the North and South Poles. These patterns are often called the Northern or Southern Lights.

Never look directly at the sun. It could make you blind. The sun is so bright and hot that you will hurt your eyes if you stare at it. Never look at the sun through a pair of binoculars or a telescope.

11

How the Sun Makes Energy

If you go out on the beach on a sunny day, you can see the sun's light and you can feel its heat. For many years, people could not figure out how the sun made all this energy. They wondered how the sun could burn for so long.

The answer is that the sun makes energy by turning hydrogen gas into helium. As it does so, it releases energy which escapes outwards into space. This process is called **nuclear fusion**.

Nature's Building Blocks

Everything in the universe is made up of the basic building blocks of nature which are called **elements**. There are 104 basic elements. Groups of elements make up everything from rocks to shoe polish.

The smallest part of an element is called an **atom**. You can think of an atom as a tiny solar system. At the center is the **nucleus**. This is made up of a cluster of **protons** and **neutrons**. Protons and neutrons are very, very small pieces of solid material. Protons contain energy. Neutrons do not. In orbit around the nucleus are a number of **electrons**. Electrons contain energy too. Under the right conditions, the energy from the protons and electrons can be released.

Nuclear Energy from the Sun

Inside the sun, it is hotter and denser than we can imagine. It is so hot and dense that nuclear fusion takes place. This happens when two atoms of hydrogen join, or fuse, together. The atoms make "heavy hydrogen," or **deuterium**. When another hydrogen atom joins on to the deuterium, it makes a helium atom. When two helium atoms collide, they make another kind of helium, and free two hydrogen atoms. The process happens again and again in a kind of chain.

Nuclear fusion releases huge amounts of energy which stream outward from the sun's core. Every second, 508 million tons of hydrogen are turned into 504 million tons of helium. The other four million tons of hydrogen are released as energy. The sun will keep shining as long as the supply of hydrogen atoms lasts.

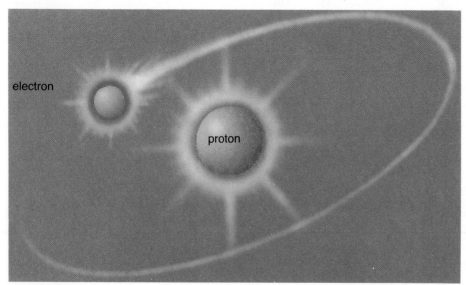

electron

proton

◄ Hydrogen is the lightest element. An atom of hydrogen has just one proton in its nucleus and one electron spinning around it.

► A hydrogen bomb, or H-bomb, explodes and releases energy. The same process happens in the sun. It is called nuclear fusion.

Rays from the Sun

Every year, a stream of energy from the sun pours down on to the earth. Each year, we get ten times more energy from the sun than is stored in all the world's unused coal and oil. This energy comes across space to the earth as **solar radiation**.

How Energy Travels

How does the radiation cross the 93 million miles to reach the earth? If you watch the sea breaking on the beach, you will see waves rolling in from far away. Energy also travels in waves. Some of the energy can be seen as light rays. Other rays cannot be seen, but they can be felt as heat. These rays have different **wavelengths**. Some of the sun's energy rays, like **ultraviolet** and **infrared**, can be harmful to living things.

The heat energy does not feel hot itself, but it warms up whatever it touches. Things feel hot when the atoms they are made up of move more quickly. The sun's energy stirs up the atoms, so they feel warmer. If you touch a car in the sunshine, it feels hot. A dark colored car will feel hotter than a white car. Dark colors take in more energy than lighter colors. This is why people paint their houses white in hot countries. Most of the sun's energy bounces off the white walls, and the people stay cool inside.

Sunlight

Sunlight looks like one color to us. We call it white light. White light is really a mixture of colors. You can see all the colors in white light when sunlight shines through raindrops to make a rainbow. The raindrops split the light up into its different parts. There are rays for each color. They travel in waves of different lengths. Blue and violet light have the shortest wavelengths. As the waves of light lengthen, we can see green light, then yellow and red.

At sunset, red skies often appear. This is because the light slants down on to the earth as the sun sets. The light travels much farther then through the gases that surround the earth than in the middle of the day when the sun is overhead. Bits of dust in the lower part of these gases scatter the light. Only the longer red and yellow waves of light get through to our eyes, so the sky looks red and yellow.

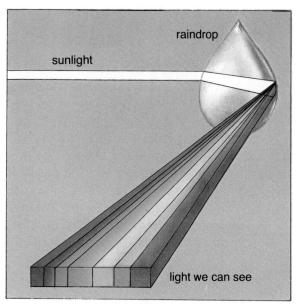

▲ When white light is split up, we see the colors of the rainbow. White light is really made of seven colors. We can only see part of the sun's radiation. We feel infrared as heat, and ultraviolet gives us a suntan.

▼ It is colder at the Poles than it is at the equator, because of the shape of the earth. The sun's rays have to pass through more of the gases that surround the earth at the Poles and so they lose heat. The land near the equator gets twice as much heat as land near the Poles.

Some parts of the earth receive more of the sun's energy than others. At the equator, the sun is high in the sky at midday all through the year. The sun's rays fall straight to the earth there. Near the North and South Poles, the rays slant down. At the Poles, energy from the sun is spread out over a larger area of the earth.

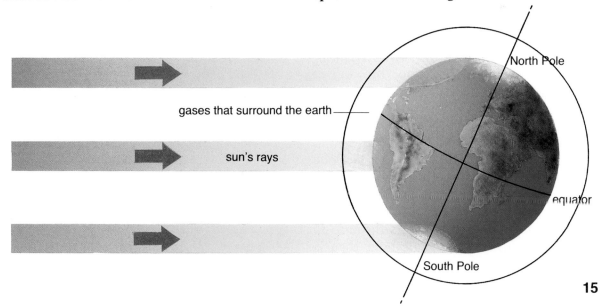

gases that surround the earth

sun's rays

North Pole

equator

South Pole

15

The Sun's Work

Everything needs energy to make it go. A bike needs the power of your legs to turn the pedals. A vacuum cleaner needs **electricity** to work its motor. The earth is the same. The sun is the earth's power plant. Without the sun, the oceans would freeze solid and the land would be so cold that life could not exist.

The "Spaceship Earth"

We are all traveling through space at over 62,000 miles per hour. The earth is our spaceship in orbit around the sun. Wrapped around the earth like a blanket is a thin layer of gases which makes up the **atmosphere**. This layer of gases is called the air. Most of the air is made of a gas called **nitrogen**. The most important gases for living things are **oxygen** and **carbon dioxide**. The atmosphere also contains water and countless bits of dust, dirt, salt from the sea, pollen grains, plant seeds, and much more.

A very important part of the atmosphere is a kind of oxygen called **ozone**. Most ozone is found in a layer about six miles above the earth's surface. The ozone layer traps a lot of the sun's ultraviolet light. If too much ultraviolet light got through to the earth, it would be dangerous to living things.

Where Does the Sun's Energy Go?

When energy from the sun reaches our atmosphere, almost a third is reflected back into space. The remainder passes through the atmosphere to the earth's surface. More solar energy gets through to the earth's surface in a single hour than is used by the whole world in a year.

The earth uses the sun's energy in all kinds of ways. The sun is the force behind our weather and climate. It creates winds, currents, and rain. It makes plants grow, gives us our food, and helps us to cook our food, too. It is also trapped in fuels like coal, gas, and oil. These fuels keep us warm, run machines to carry us around, and make our factories work.

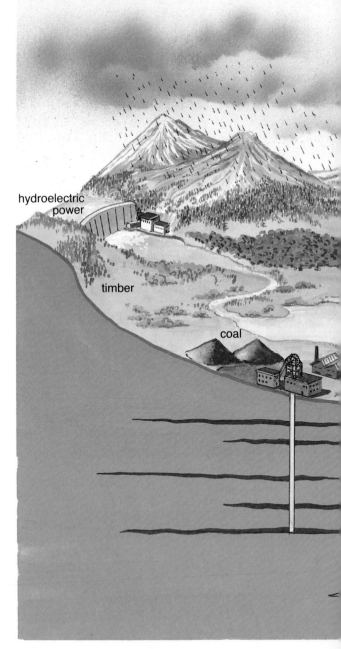

hydroelectric power

timber

coal

▼ **Only a little of the sun's energy reaches the earth's atmosphere. Without the sun our world would be a dead planet.**

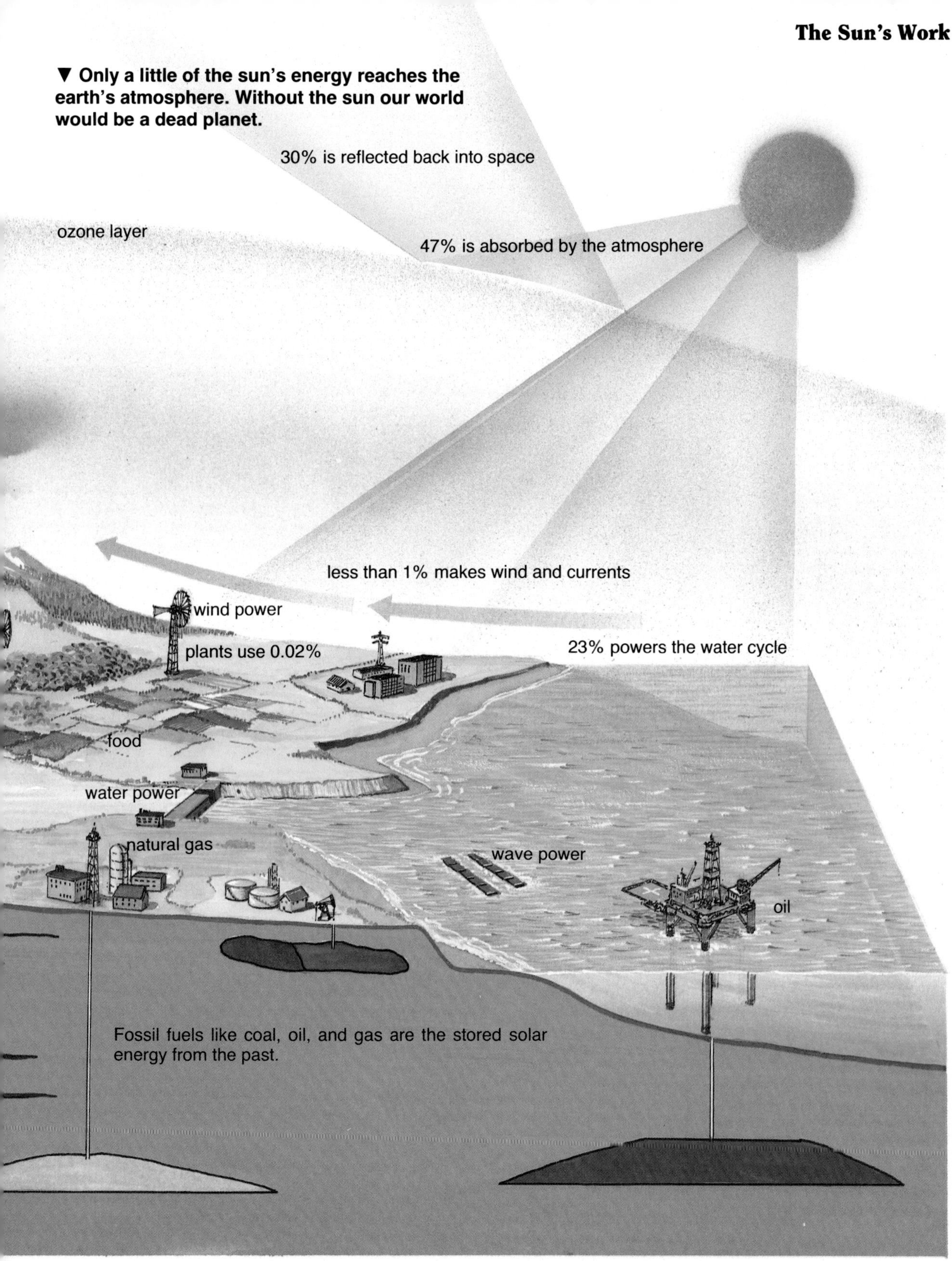

30% is reflected back into space

ozone layer

47% is absorbed by the atmosphere

less than 1% makes wind and currents

wind power

plants use 0.02%

23% powers the water cycle

food

water power

natural gas

wave power

oil

Fossil fuels like coal, oil, and gas are the stored solar energy from the past.

The Weather Machine

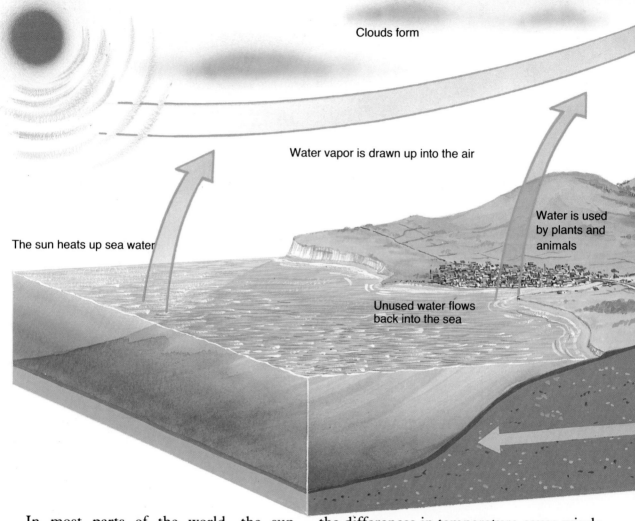

Clouds form

Water vapor is drawn up into the air

The sun heats up sea water

Water is used by plants and animals

Unused water flows back into the sea

In most parts of the world, the sun shines more in the summer, and it feels hotter than it does in winter. However, there is more to our weather and climate than that.

Winds

The sun does not heat up every place on the earth to the same temperature. For example, it is cooler at the Poles than at the equator. This is important because the differences in temperature cause winds. As air is heated up by the sun, it rises, and cooler air rushes in to take its place. This movement of air is called wind. Some winds form a regular pattern all over the world. Sailors knew that some special winds would always blow at the same time of year. They relied on these winds to help them get their goods to port on time. Sailors called these regular patterns of winds the Trade Winds.

18

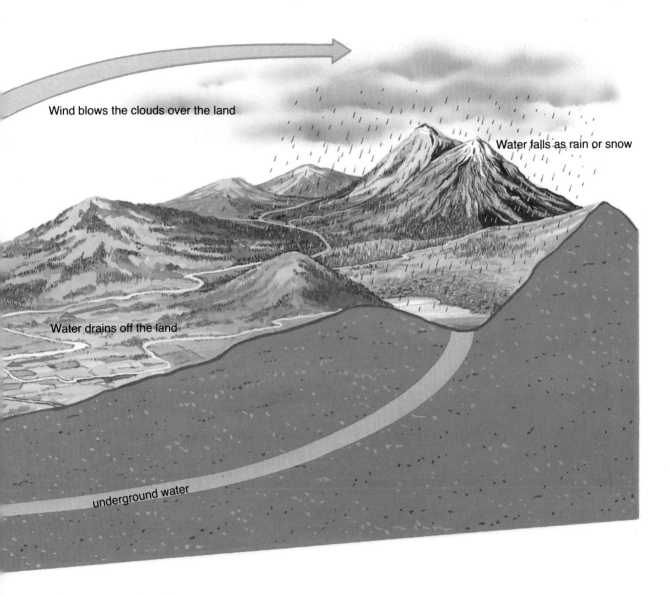

Wind blows the clouds over the land

Water falls as rain or snow

Water drains off the land

underground water

The Water Cycle

Water is vital for all living things. Most of the world's water is found in the seas and oceans, but seawater is too salty to drink. Only a small part of the world's water is found in the lakes, rivers, and streams. This store of water would soon be used up if it were not for the power of the sun.

Sunshine heats up the seawater. This makes some of the water turn into **water vapor**, leaving the salt behind. The water vapor rises up into the air and forms clouds. Winds may blow the clouds over the land. As the clouds rise, they cool. The water vapor then turns back into drops of water. The drops of fresh water fall on the land as rain.

Some of the rain water is used by plants and animals. Some drains into the lakes and rivers. Any water which has not been used flows back into the sea. Then, the whole process begins again.

19

The Green Planet

People have always dreamed of finding life out in space. So far, we have had no success. The reason why the earth is a green and living planet is that it has a special place in the solar system. It is not so close to the sun that it is scorched like Mercury. Nor is it so far away that it is a frozen waste like Pluto. It gets just the right amount of energy from the sun so that living things can grow.

The other vital thing about the earth is its atmosphere. The atmosphere contains oxygen, which all living things need to breathe. The atmosphere had very little oxygen in it when the earth was first formed. We could not have lived in those clouds of deadly gases. The first plants on the earth began to change the air. They gave off oxygen which made it possible for animal life to exist.

Food Factories

A plant gives off oxygen while it makes its food. The plant roots take up water from the soil. The leaves take in carbon dioxide from the air. The plant uses

◄ All living things use energy from the sun. These people are working on a banana farm. Bananas need a lot of sunshine to grow. The people will sell the fruit to buy food and other goods.

sunlight to turn the water and carbon dioxide into sugar, which is the plant's food. Oxygen is then given off through the leaves. This whole process is called **photosynthesis**, which means "making with light."

Scientists have tried to copy the way plants trap the sun's energy. They understand how photosynthesis works, but they cannot copy it in a way that would give us a useful amount of energy.

Photosynthesis happens in the parts of the plant called **chloroplasts**. You can think of chloroplasts as tiny green factories in the plant's leaves. The power that makes these factories work is sunlight.

Food Chains

As well as giving us oxygen to breathe, plants give us food. Many plants are eaten by animals. These animals, in turn, may become food for other animals. (People eat a mixture of plants and animals.) These stages link together to make up a food chain. Food chains often join or cross other chains, but the starting point is always the plants. There would be no animal life without plants. There would be no plants without sunlight.

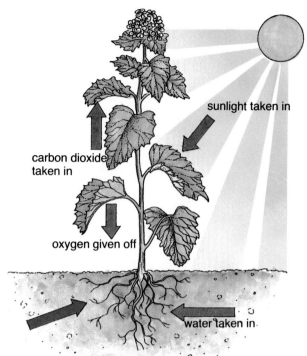

carbon dioxide taken in

sunlight taken in

oxygen given off

water taken in

▲ All green plants need sunlight. They use it to make their food by a process called photosynthesis.

▼ Each time something is eaten in a food chain, energy is taken in by the feeder. There is less energy in the food at the end of the chain. People and some animals eat from many different chains. When chains are linked together, they are called a food web.

Our Changing Atmosphere

▼ Waste gases are given off when fossil fuels burn. These wastes may damage, or pollute, the environment.

When the earth was young, 4.5 billion years ago, violent storms raged. Volcanoes threw out dust and ash. It was scorching hot and the atmosphere contained a lot of carbon dioxide.

The thick layer of carbon dioxide let in the energy from the sun, but it kept heat from getting back out into space. When the first simple plants started to use carbon dioxide, the atmosphere changed. With less carbon dioxide in the atmosphere, the planet lost some of its heat. The first animals started to grow. They fed on plants and breathed oxygen from the air.

Burning Fossil Fuels

Most of the energy we use today comes from burning the fossil fuels coal, oil, and gas. As they burn, they give off carbon dioxide as well as heat. As more and more fossil fuels are burned, more and more carbon dioxide builds up in the atmosphere. Just as it did at the beginning of the world, carbon dioxide keeps heat from escaping out into space. This is called the **greenhouse effect**.

If you stand inside a greenhouse on a sunny day, it feels hotter than it does outside. This is because waves of **radiant**

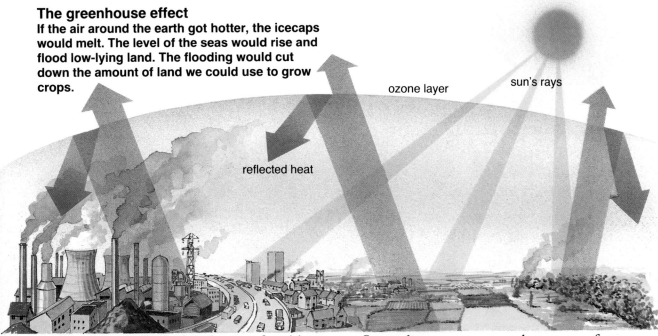

The greenhouse effect
If the air around the earth got hotter, the icecaps would melt. The level of the seas would rise and flood low-lying land. The flooding would cut down the amount of land we could use to grow crops.

ozone layer

sun's rays

reflected heat

energy pass through the glass roof and heat up the air inside the greenhouse. The radiant heat inside the greenhouse has a longer wavelength, so not so much bounces back out through the glass.

Some scientists believe that the greenhouse effect is slowly heating up our planet. The atmosphere around Venus is almost all carbon dioxide. The greenhouse effect there makes the temperature near the ground as high as 900°F. This is almost twice as hot as the hottest kitchen oven.

Here on the earth, it might get just a few degrees hotter in the next hundred years. This would be enough to change the climate, and it might make the ice in the polar regions melt.

Disappearing Forests

Much of the land on the earth used to be covered by forests. Slowly, trees have been cleared to make room for towns and cities, farms, and factories.

Trees are vital to us because they make oxygen. They also help us to use up the carbon dioxide given off when fossil fuels burn.

It makes sense to take care of our forests, but it is not easy. We use wood in all kinds of ways. We use it for building and for making fences, paper, and furniture. We also use it for heating. Even where wood is not used, trees are cut down to make more room for people to live and grow food.

▲ We need trees to keep the right balance of gases in our atmosphere. We must not chop down too many trees. If we do, there will not be enough oxygen in the air.

23

Solar Energy Worldwide

When people talk about using solar energy, they mean finding ways of using the sun's energy directly. A simple example is when we hang out washing on the line to dry in the sunshine.

The energy of the sun has been used by people for a long time. Over 3,000 years

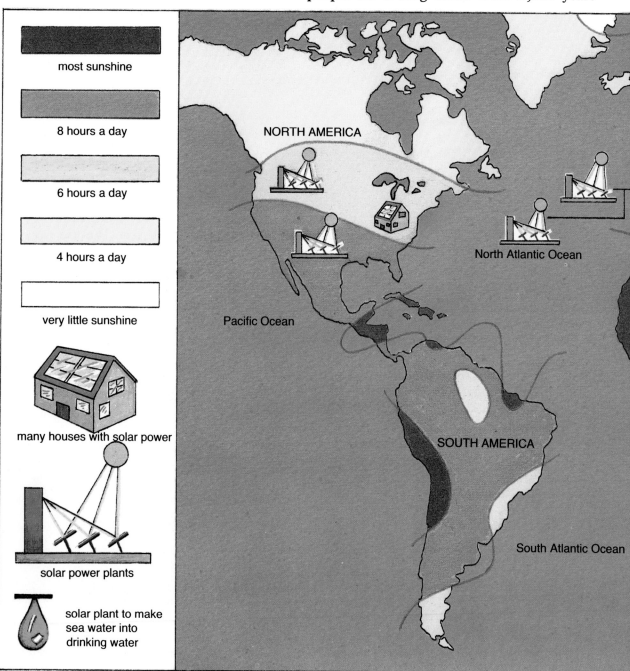

most sunshine

8 hours a day

6 hours a day

4 hours a day

very little sunshine

many houses with solar power

solar power plants

solar plant to make sea water into drinking water

NORTH AMERICA

North Atlantic Ocean

Pacific Ocean

SOUTH AMERICA

South Atlantic Ocean

ago, a king's palace in Turkey was warmed with water heated by the sun. The first place for collecting the sun's energy, or **solar furnace**, was built in France in 1714. In 1878, a solar steam engine was used to drive a printing press in Paris.

One problem with using solar energy is that the sun does not shine for the same length of time all over the world. Also, scientists do not yet know the best way of trapping the energy of the sun. At the moment, a large city might need so many solar collectors to power it that they might take up as much land as the city itself.

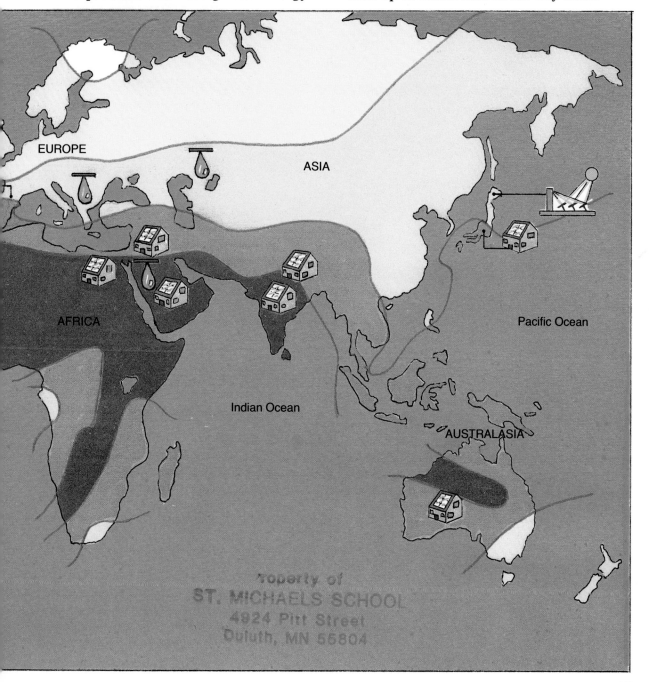

Ancient Beliefs

▼ This painting is more than 2,000 years old. It is on the coffin of an Egyptian. The sun is giving life and warmth to the dead body. The Egyptians thought that people went on to another life after they had died.

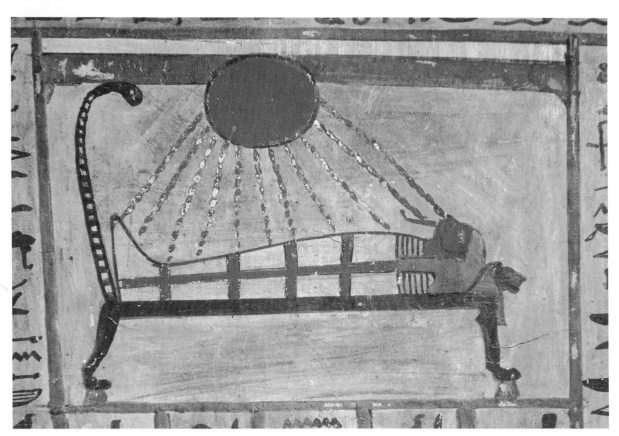

People have known about the power of the sun since very early times. It brought light in the morning. It gave them warmth. It made their crops grow. They did not understand how this happened. They thought it was magic. They came to think of the sun as a god.

We know from writings and pictures that the sun was worshipped in many countries. In India, the sun god was called Savitr, which means "giver of life." In northern countries, the winter is long. Many days pass when the sun shines only for a short time or not at all. Festivals were held in midwinter to ask for the return of the sun. Even now, midsummer day is special to the people who live in the north of Europe. The sun shines for the longest time then, and the dark days of winter seem far away.

The Sun God in Ancient Egypt

In Egypt, the sun shines strongly for most of the year. The sun brings life and death. It helps to make crops grow, but too much sun dries up the ground and the crops die.

Five thousand years ago, many gods and goddesses were worshipped in Egypt. Most of them took the form of animals, but one of the most powerful was the sun god. People believed that the sun god brought light and life to the world. The sun god was given different names for different times of the day. In the morning, he was called Khepri, the scarab beetle. When he came to full strength at midday, he was Re or Ra. In the evening, at the time of his death, he was an old man, Atum.

For one Egyptian king, the sun became so important that he told the people to worship only the sun god. This god had only one name, which was Aten. The king built a great new temple to Aten. It was different from the other temples because it was open and allowed the sun's rays to come streaming in.

▼ The Mayan people built this temple to the sun in Mexico over 1,000 years ago.

South and Central America

The Incas lived in South America. They believed that the sun god created the first Inca on an island in Lake Titicaca on the borders of Bolivia and Peru. In Central America, the Mayan people built large temples to the gods of the sun and the moon. These temples were built with giant steps leading up to the top of the building.

The Aztecs also lived in Central America. They were fierce hunters who worshipped gods of the sky. The Aztecs believed that their gods brought good or bad luck, sickness or health, and victory or defeat in war. The Aztecs also built temples to their gods. They believed that the gods made the sun rise and set. If the sun was not fed with offerings, it might disappear from the sky. People have slowly begun to understand how the sun works, and they no longer see it as a god.

Using Energy

The first people lived on the food that they hunted or gathered. They cooked it, and kept themselves warm by burning wood. Later, they found other ways of using energy to make their lives easier. They used tamed animals to help them carry or pull things. Wind and water mills helped them do their work much more quickly.

The Steam Revolution

In 1777, James Watt, a Scottish engineer, invented a steam pumping engine. He soon made his engine move things around and around as well as up and down. Before long, engineers had learned how to use steam to power machines which could carry things, too.

In 1825, the first passenger steam train was built. The train was called *Locomotion*, and it reached a speed of fifteen miles per hour on its forty mile journey.

The demand for steam engines grew. Factories were set up to make the steel to build the engines. People moved to the towns to work in the factories. The way of life of many people changed forever.

Wood powered the early steam engines, but wood was very bulky to store. When people started to dig coal out of the ground, coal was used instead of wood.

Emptying the Store

All the coal, oil, and gas in the world was formed about 400 million years ago. These fossil fuels are being used up much faster than new fuel is being formed. We do not know exactly how much fossil fuel

▼ Animals have been used to supply energy since early times. Machines can work harder than animals. Machines do not get tired.

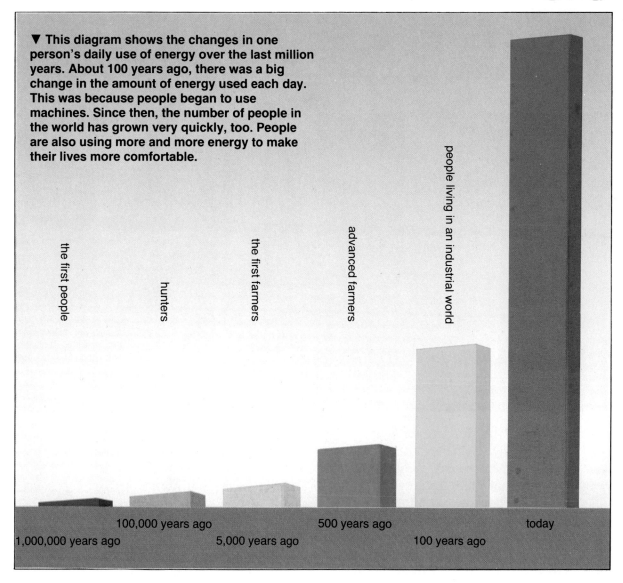

▼ This diagram shows the changes in one person's daily use of energy over the last million years. About 100 years ago, there was a big change in the amount of energy used each day. This was because people began to use machines. Since then, the number of people in the world has grown very quickly, too. People are also using more and more energy to make their lives more comfortable.

the first people

hunters

the first farmers

advanced farmers

people living in an industrial world

1,000,000 years ago

100,000 years ago

5,000 years ago

500 years ago

100 years ago

today

is left. Scientists estimate that we have enough coal left to last us for more than a thousand years. Oil and gas are in much shorter supply. If we go on using them as we do now, they will probably run out in the next hundred years.

Most of the world's energy is used in places like the US, Japan, and Europe. In other areas, like Africa and India, many people live more simply. Their energy needs are smaller. However, they are beginning to use more energy as they build more factories and use more machines.

People always want to travel farther and faster, and they want to live more comfortably. This means that our energy needs double every ten years.

People have started just recently to do something about this **energy crisis**. We are now beginning to save energy by doing such things as building houses which have **insulation**. This means that the walls, roof, and floors of an insulated house are lined with materials which do not allow heat to pass out through them easily. However, we need to find more ways to save energy.

Power from Plants

▼ Brazil has to buy gasoline from other countries. Sugar cane grows well in Brazil. Many cars run on alcohol made from sugar cane, instead of using gasoline.

Plants store the sun's energy in their stalks and leaves. Some of this energy is passed to us when we eat plants. Another way of releasing plant energy is to use plants as fuel. Plant fuel is called **biomass**.

Coal is made of the remains of plants which lived millions of years ago. There is no need to wait this long to use plants for fuel. The most common form of biomass is wood. Wood was burned all over the world before fossil fuels were discovered.

In some countries, like China and India, many people rely on wood for all their cooking and heating. In these parts of the world, biomass is important.

Wood could not supply industry with all the energy it needs, but it is again being used in some countries to heat homes. In Norway and Sweden, one tenth of the houses use wood-burning stoves.

Some countries do not have stocks of oil and coal, and they cannot afford to buy them. If they have large forests, wood may be the only fuel they can use. Sri Lanka and Tanzania now use wood for industry, as well as in their homes.

Gasoline from Plants

Most cars run on gasoline or diesel. Both of these fuels are made from oil, which is only found in some parts of the world. Countries which do not have their own supplies of oil have been looking for other fuels to use.

Plants rich in sugar, like sugar cane, can be treated to make fuel. The fuel is made by **fermenting** the sugar cane. It is like making beer. Natural yeasts work on the sugar cane and turn it into alcohol.

Vegetable oils also make a good fuel. The oils from crushed seeds and nuts such as sunflower, peanut, soya, and palm have all been used as fuels by themselves. They have also been mixed with other fuels.

Growing Fuel

It would need very large areas of land to grow enough plants to supply fuel for a power plant. There are problems when land is used for fuel instead of food. In Brazil, a lot of land near big cities is used to grow sugar cane. The sugar cane is turned into fuel. When the land is used for sugar cane, people cannot grow their own food. It is important to have a balance between growing fuel and growing food.

One answer might be to use wasteland. Some simple plants grow easily anywhere as long as there is sunlight and some water. One type of these plants is **algae**. Algae can be grown in special tanks which can be set up in the desert where nothing else can grow. Seaweed and water hyacinths can be grown in the lakes and seas, and these plants can be made into fuel.

▼ Some farmers burn straw after the harvest. This is a waste of energy. Some farmers now burn the straw in a furnace. The burning straw gives off heat to run farm machines in dairies, and to dry grain.

▲ These people are collecting seaweed from the sea in Spain. It is used in the chemical industry.

Gas from Plants

Another way of using plants for fuel is to turn them into **biogas**. It is made when plants and animal droppings, or **dung**, rot. Biogas can be used in stoves for cooking. It can also be used for heating and lighting or to make electricity.

Biogas is very useful in places where there is very little firewood. On treeless plains in parts of India, people use dried dung as fuel. When dung is all burned up, there is no fertilizer to go back on to the soil. Crops do not grow well without fertilizer. Instead of being burned, the dung could be used to make biogas. Then, the leftover material could be put on the fields as fertilizer.

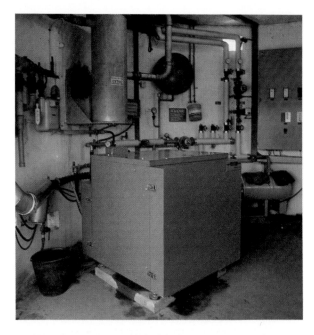

▲ Simple biogas containers are dug into the ground. Some farms have larger machines like this one. The gas is stored until it is needed. The waste is put back on the fields.

◀ Animal droppings are dried in the sun outside a village in Kurdistan, Southwest Asia. When the dung is dry, it is used as a fuel on the villagers' fires.

How Biogas is Made

Biogas is made in a container. It must be airtight and warm. It should be heated to about body temperature. The best mixture for making biogas is human or animal waste, and some plant waste. Bacteria break down, or **digest**, the waste. A gas that is mostly **methane** is given off. The gas goes into a storage chamber, and is ready to be used.

A Chinese Village

One fifth of the world's people live in China. Most of them live in villages. The people grow their own food and sell any extra to their neighbors. They also try to supply some of their own energy needs.

Fifty years ago, many people in China were starving. The Chinese had to grow more food. They started to reuse, or **recycle**, materials and not waste anything. One way of doing this is to make biogas. There are now about seven million biogas containers in China. They run mainly on waste from houses. In some of the villages, fast-growing plants like water hyacinths and napier grass are grown to make biogas. Up to two fifths of the electricity used by a village may come from biogas.

Gas from Garbage

Garbage is often buried in deep pits. As it rots, it gives off a gas that is rich in methane. This gas can be collected and used as fuel. In America, there are over thirty of these landfill gas sites.

In the future, we may see energy farms instead of coal mines and oil rigs. One answer to the energy crisis might be to grow our way out of it.

▼ China is the world leader in using biogas. This type of energy is cheap. It does not have to be brought to the villages by long-distance pipelines.

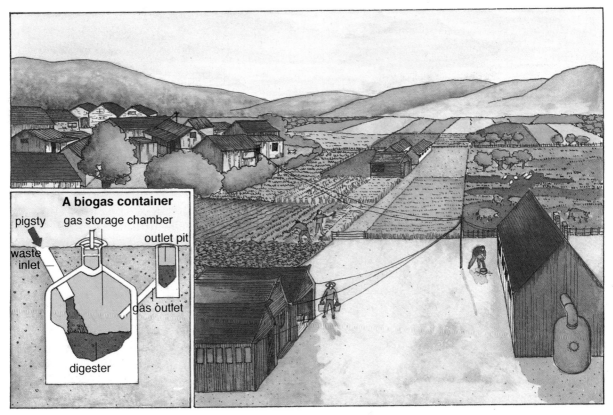

A biogas container

pigsty
gas storage chamber
outlet pit
waste inlet
gas outlet
digester

Using the Sun's Rays

▼ This solar power station is in Sicily. The rows of mirrors focus the sun's heat on to the top of the tower. In the front of the picture, you can see the electrical plant.

The sunlight shining down on the earth contains thousands of times more energy than we need. The problem is how to harness it. The sun does not always give us heat when we need it. There is less sunshine in the winter when we need heat for our houses. It is difficult to store the energy for the times when we want to use it.

There are two main ways of using solar energy. The first turns sunshine straight into electricity. The second collects the heat and stores it.

Sunshine to Electricity

A solar furnace collects the sun's heat on a large scale. The sunshine is focused on a central point. The point gets as hot as 1,650°F. The heat is then carried away to work **generators**, which make electricity.

The solar furnace in Odeillo, France has sixty-three flat mirrors. The mirrors turn automatically as they follow the sun across the sky. The mirrors focus the sun's rays on to the furnace. The furnace makes heat of up to 5,400°F.

The largest solar power plant built so far is in California. It has 1,818 mirrors arranged in a circle around a central tower full of oil. When the oil is heated by the sun, it flows away to work a generator.

The equipment needed to build solar power plants is still very expensive. Once solar power plants are built, they have three advantages: there is very little that can go wrong; solar power plants do not **pollute** the air with poisonous wastes; and the energy that works them will not run out!

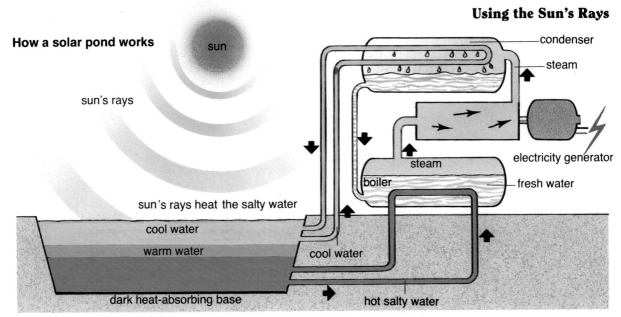

How a solar pond works

sun

sun's rays

condenser

steam

electricity generator

steam

boiler

fresh water

sun's rays heat the salty water

cool water

warm water

cool water

dark heat-absorbing base

hot salty water

Collecting Sunshine

A **solar pond** collects and stores heat. The pond has a flat, black bottom. It is filled with salty water, which absorbs heat better than freshwater. The pond is saltiest at the bottom. As the sun shines, the water at the bottom of the pond gets very hot. The hot salt water is pumped through pipes to a boiler. The heat from the hot salt water pipes heats up freshwater in the boiler. The freshwater turns to steam which works an electrical generator. The steam **condenses** back into water, and the whole process begins again.

Fresh Water from the Sun

In deserts, there is often a shortage of drinking water, but there might be plenty of seawater close by. The water in the sea is turned into water vapor in a **solar still**. As the water vapor rises, it leaves behind the salt. When the hot water vapor touches a cold surface, it condenses into freshwater, which is ready for drinking.

▶ Solar ponds only work where there is plenty of sunshine. This one is near the Dead Sea in Israel.

35

Solar Homes

Even the earliest people used the sun to help keep them warm. They chose caves to live in which had entrances facing the strongest sun of the day. Today, in cold countries, it is a good idea to build houses facing south to make the most of what sunshine there is. In hot countries, houses face away from the sun and have small windows to help keep them cool inside.

Sunshine already helps to heat our homes. As it streams in through the windows, it gives us more than one fifth of the heat we need. In the winter, most of this heat passes out again and is lost.

▼ The white walls of this house in Greece reflect the sun's energy away from the building. The shutters stop the sunshine from streaming in through the windows. The shutters and white walls help to keep the house cool.

Solar Storage

The sun's energy can be used more directly to heat houses. The problem is to store the heat when the sun shines, so that it can be used when the weather is colder or at night.

Solar panels are a simple way of turning sunshine into heat. They are attached to the roofs or walls of houses. The bottom of a panel is black to absorb as much heat as possible. A length of pipe containing water is coiled up along the panel, and the whole panel is covered with glass. The sun warms up the water in the pipes, which can then go straight to the hot water supply. To store the heat, the water flows away to a tank under the house. This tank is surrounded by special rocks which are warmed by the hot water. When the weather gets cold, air is pumped through the rocks. The air warms up and then heats the rest of the house.

Solar panels work best in hot countries. Even in cooler places, they can cut heating bills by fifty percent or more.

Making the Most of Solar Energy

In some places, people are adding special equipment to their houses to use solar energy for heating. In other places, new houses can be built which include equipment for solar power.

In a solar house, the windows face south to let in as much sunshine as possible. Solar collectors on the roof or built into the walls store the sun's heat for use when it gets cold.

There is no point in putting heat into a building if it just leaks away again. That is like pouring water into a bucket full of holes. To work well, solar houses are built so that they lose as little heat as possible. The roofs, walls, and windows have to be well insulated.

A solar house costs more than an ordinary one to build. But when it is finished, it costs the people who live in it very little to run. The sun's energy is free and it will not run out. Other forms of energy, like coal and oil, have to be delivered and paid for all the time.

▲ Winter sunshine is strong enough to heat water for homes. These solar panels in Switzerland make hot water even when the weather is very cold.

▼ The solar panels on the right and the drums on the walls on the left collect the sun's heat for this house in the United States. The big shutters on the ground cover the drums when energy is not needed.

Solar Collectors

Solar cells are different from solar panels. They turn sunlight straight into electricity.

Solar cells were first used in America in the 1950s. They are expensive compared with the amount of energy they make. Here on the earth, they only turn about one tenth of the sun's energy that falls on them into electricity. However, they are getting cheaper as more of them are being made.

How They Work

Solar cells are usually made of **silicon**. Beach sand is made of silicon. Therefore, silicon is a very common substance. The sun's rays contain **electromagnetic energy**. When the rays fall on a solar cell, they free electrons from the silicon atoms. The electrons flow away as electricity. Each cell makes a very small amount of electricity. Large groups of solar cells, called **arrays**, have to be used to make a useful amount of energy.

Out in space, there are no clouds or atmosphere to block out the sun's rays. This is why solar cells are used widely to power the instruments carried by spacecraft.

◄ **Rows of solar cells make electricity at a power plant in the desert. They work only where the sun is hot all year round.**

Transportation

Solar cells have been tried in all kinds of vehicles. In 1981, a light plastic plane called *Solar Challenger* flew from Paris in France to England in five and a half hours. The plane was powered by 16,000 solar cells on its wings and tail.

In 1986, a solar car called *Sunrider* was driven from Athens in Greece to Lisbon in Portugal. It was powered by 300 solar cells, and it traveled at under twenty miles per hour. When the sun went down, extra power stored in its batteries was used.

Large numbers of solar cells are needed to power these types of vehicles. In the future, as technology advances, solar cells should become more efficient.

Other Uses

Solar cells have no moving parts, and they do not need much care. They are useful in places without an energy supply or are a long way from the supply.

In remote villages in Africa and Asia, solar cells are used to run refrigerators for medical supplies. They make power for pumping water, running lights, and working telephones. The lights on buoys far out at sea are often solar-powered. Pocket calculators and watches often run on solar cells now. Solar cells mean that we can use the sun's energy in many more ways.

▲ A telephone does not need much electricity. The solar cells in the panel above the telephone box are used to power this telephone in Tasmania.

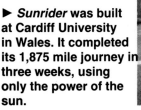

▶ *Sunrider* was built at Cardiff University in Wales. It completed its 1,875 mile journey in three weeks, using only the power of the sun.

Power Plants in Space

▼ Solar power plants have to be very large to supply energy to the earth. Spacecraft could carry the parts out into space. There is no gravity in space, so moving such huge structures would not be as difficult as it is here on earth.

Two facts led to the idea of building a power plant in space. First, most of the sun's energy does not reach the earth. The atmosphere and the clouds stop the energy from getting through.

Secondly, there is no shortage of room in space. If towns and cities wanted to use solar energy, they would need a vast number of solar cells covering huge areas of land.

Building a Power Plant

Space scientists first thought about putting a power plant in space in the 1960s. At first, people thought the idea was impossible. Then, fossil fuel supplies began to run low. Scientists had to look for other ways of keeping up with the world's energy needs.

A solar power plant would have huge arrays of solar cells. They would be as much as twenty miles square and carry millions of solar cells. The parts would have to be made on the earth and then taken bit by bit into space.

Transmission to Earth

Scientists think that the sun's energy could be collected as rays called **microwaves**. Then, a giant antenna would send the microwaves down to the earth. Microwaves pass through clouds easily. Therefore, little energy would be lost on the way. On the earth, huge receivers, covering fifty square miles of land or more would collect the microwaves.

No solar power plants have been built in space yet. There are many problems to be solved before we will be able to see one in the night sky. Microwaves would be dangerous if they missed their targets. They would scorch the land they hit. They might also get in the way of radio waves, and the microwave receivers would take up a lot of land.

▼ **In the future, solar power plants might be used to refuel spacecraft. Scientists think that a spacecraft flight could last for much longer if it could refuel from a fuel supply in space.**

Copying the Sun

In the core of the sun, millions of tons of hydrogen are turned into millions of tons of helium every second. The energy freed by this nuclear fusion streams out into space. For years, scientists have tried to copy it. If they manage to overcome all the problems, we might one day have power plants on the earth which work like tiny suns.

Controlling the Energy

Scientists use two kinds of hydrogen to make nuclear fusion take place. One is deuterium and the other is **tritium**. The hydrogen atoms have to be squeezed together at very high temperatures. This makes a new element, helium, and releases large amounts of energy. If the energy is

▼ Atoms of deuterium and tritium join together to form a new element, helium. At the same time, a spare neutron escapes.

released all at once, there is an explosion. This has been done to make the hydrogen bomb. There are two problems with fusion. It is very difficult to control. It is also difficult to reach the high temperatures at which the atoms will fuse.

Making Fusion

Deep inside the sun, it is 25 million °F. On the earth, it has to be even hotter for fusion to happen. At such high temperatures, very hot gas called **plasma** is made. The plasma has to be put under great pressure by squeezing it. The problem is how to contain and squeeze the plasma. The walls of any ordinary container would just melt away.

One answer might be to use a device which makes walls you cannot see. It is called a **Tokamak reactor**. It uses magnetism to make powerful **magnetic fields** which hold and squeeze the plasma. Tokamak reactors were invented in the USSR. A record temperature of 360 million °F has been reached in a Tokamak, but it lasted for less than half a second. Even so, this was long enough to release a large amount of energy.

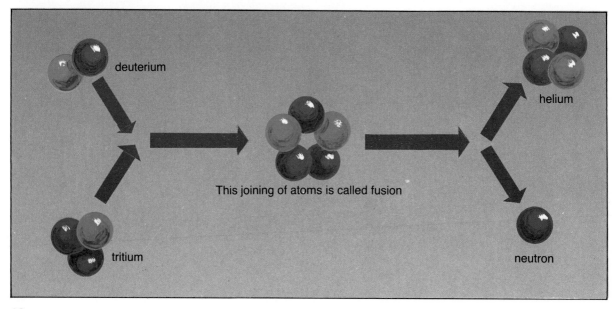

deuterium

helium

This joining of atoms is called fusion

tritium

neutron

▶ This hydrogen atom is being heated. The computer picture shows that the red center is getting very hot. If the atom is heated to 180 million °F for long enough, fusion would take place.

▼ The biggest Tokamak reactors are in the United States, Britain and Japan. They can reach temperatures ten times higher than the heat in the sun.

Fusion by Rays

Powerful beams of light known as **lasers** can also set off fusion. Laser beams are fired at tiny pieces of deuterium and tritium. This method is not very efficient because the lasers use more energy than the fusion process releases.

The Fuel of the Future?

It looks as though nuclear fusion could be safer than **nuclear fission**. Nuclear fission is another kind of nuclear power. During nuclear fission, atoms are split, not fused, to make energy. Nuclear fission also gives off harmful rays. The main waste in fusion is in the harmless gas, helium.

Another good thing about fusion is that the hydrogen needed is found in water. We are certainly not in danger of running out of water. So, if all the problems can be solved, nuclear fusion would give us an almost endless energy supply.

Looking Ahead

At the moment, we get less than one percent of our energy from the sun, but this will increase. Scientists are finding new ways of using the sun. Already, it supplies energy to some places far away from power lines and roads. In California, complete solar power plants are being built. The plan is that the sun will supply all the extra electricity needed in California for the next ten years or more.

▼ The oceans store heat from the sun. Water is often 36° warmer at the surface than on the seabed.

Using the Oceans

The oceans cover about three quarters of the earth's surface. Much of the sun's energy falls on the oceans, which makes them the biggest solar collectors of all. There is an exciting idea for tapping the warmth stored in seawater. It is called OTEC, which stands for Ocean Thermal Energy Converter.

An OTEC power plant works because the seawater near the surface is warmer than the water deep down. An OTEC plant contains a liquid gas called **ammonia**. In the warm water near the surface, the ammonia boils and turns into vapor. The moving gas turns the blades in a generator to make electricity. The ammonia gas is then cooled with cold water from the seabed. As the gas cools, it condenses back into liquid and the cycle begins again.

An OTEC plant is being tested in the warm waters off the coast of Hawaii. Full size plants would be as big as oil rigs. They would supply enough power for whole cities. So far, no one knows what effect OTEC plants would have on life in the oceans around them. An ammonia leak could cause great harm.

Saving Energy

Our way of life makes us use a lot of energy very quickly. Our fossil fuel supplies are being used up. Although nuclear power plants can supply large amounts of energy, many people are worried about how safe they are.

Someday, the sun could fulfill all our energy needs. Until then, we must use our fuel supply carefully. Low-energy houses make the best use of fuel. Having good home insulation and wearing extra clothing are ways to keep, or **conserve**, energy.

Recycling materials helps to save energy. Items like old paper, used metal, or broken glass are collected and used again instead of being thrown away. It uses less energy to recycle the material than it does to make the paper, metal, or glass in the first place.

The Solar Age

Solar power is not a cheap form of power yet, but it has many good points. Unlike fossil fuel, it does not send poisonous gases into the atmosphere. Unlike nuclear power, there is no danger from harmful rays. Best of all, it will be another five billion years before the sun stops shining!

▶ We have to get rid of our garbage. In some places, garbage is collected and taken to a special plant. There, it is burned and the heat is pumped back to heat houses and offices.

Glossary

algae: very simple plants. Algae have no leaves, roots, or stems. Most algae are found in water.

ammonia: a gas with no color but a strong smell. It is often used in liquid form.

array: a number of objects or instruments laid out so they can be seen easily, or so that the sun can shine on them.

atmosphere: the layer of gases that surrounds a planet. The earth's atmosphere is the air.

atom: the smallest part of a substance that can still behave like that substance.

big bang theory: a scientific idea that everything in the universe started with a very large explosion. It is thought that everything in the universe is still moving away from the center of the explosion.

biogas: a gas made when plant and animal wastes rot without the presence of air.

biomass: when plant material is used for fuel.

carbon dioxide: a gas found in the air. All animals breathe out carbon dioxide. Plants use carbon dioxide to make food.

chloroplasts: green plant cells in which the plant's food is made.

chromosphere: a layer of hot gases that makes up part of the sun's atmosphere. It has a pinkish color.

condense: to turn a gas into a liquid.

conserve: to protect or use something carefully so that it is not wasted or does not run out.

convective zone: the outer part of the sun where currents of hot gas whirl around. This movement helps the sun's energy to escape.

core: the center. Energy is made in the sun's core.

corona: a thin, hot layer of gas surrounding the sun.

deuterium: a form of the gas hydrogen. Deuterium is very common in seawater.

digest: to break down a material such as food into simpler parts. It is done by bacteria in some cases.

dung: waste matter from animals. It contains material that is good for the soil.

electricity: a kind of energy which can travel along wires. It is used to heat and light homes, run factories, and work many machines.

electromagnetic energy: something that has both electric and magnetic forces. Radio waves, ultraviolet, infrared, and X-rays are all electromagnetic.

electron: a particle outside the center of an atom which has a negative electrical charge.

elements: the different basic materials from which everything in the universe is made.

energy: the power to do work; what makes things go.

energy crisis: a situation where the world's fuel reserves are running out and new supplies are needed to replace them.

fermentation: when yeasts work on plant material to make alcohol.

flare: a burst of energy which makes a bright area on the sun's surface.

fossil fuel: fuel made millions of years ago by the action of heat and pressure on plant and animal remains. Fossil fuels are coal, oil, and gas.

fuel: material which is used up when energy is released.

galaxy: a very large group of stars. Together the galaxies make up the universe.

generator: a machine for changing mechanical energy into electrical energy.

gravity: the force that pulls everything towards the center of a planet. The earth's gravity makes objects fall and gives them weight.

greenhouse effect: the heating up of the earth's atmosphere. The atmosphere acts like the glass in a greenhouse by not allowing some of the heat from the sun's rays to escape.

helium: a light gas found in air and in the sun.

hydrogen: a very light gas. The sun is made up of hydrogen gas.

infrared: rays which are longer than the red light waves we can see, but shorter than radio waves. We feel them as heat.

insulation: materials used in building which stop or slow down the rate at which heat passes through them.

kinetic energy: the energy in something when it moves.

lasers: a machine which produces a beam of very strong light. The beams can be very thin. They are used in industry and medicine.

light-year: the distance light travels in a year which is 5.9 trillion miles. The sun is just eight light minutes from the earth.

magnetic field: an area of force like that around a magnet.

methane: a gas formed by decaying animal and plant matter. It can be used as fuel.

microwave: a radio wave with a very short wavelength. It stirs up the molecules of water in objects, making them hot. Microwaves can be used to cook things.

neutron: a particle in the center of an atom which has no electrical charge.

nitrogen: a gas found in all living things. It has no color, smell, or taste. It does not burn.

nuclear fission: the process of splitting atoms that takes place in nuclear power plants.

nuclear fusion: the process of fusing atoms that takes place inside the sun.

nucleus: the center of an atom.

orbit: the path of one body, like a planet or a satellite, around another body. The earth moves in orbit around the sun.

oxygen: a gas found in air and water. Oxygen is very important to all plants and animals. We cannot breathe without oxygen.

ozone: a kind of oxygen. It is part of the earth's atmosphere. It is found in a layer about six miles above the surface.

photosphere: the surface of the sun that we can see. It is made of hot gases and gives off almost all the light we get from the sun.

photosynthesis: the way plants make food. Using energy from sunlight, plants turn carbon dioxide and water into sugars. Oxygen is given off.

planet: a body in space which moves in orbit around a star like the sun.

plasma: a hot, electrically charged gas. It is like the material that makes up the sun.

pollute: to dirty or poison the air, land, or water. Air pollution is caused by waste chemicals from factories or by gases made when fossil fuels are burned.

proton: a particle in the center of an atom with a positive electric charge.

radiant energy: energy that is given out in waves, or radiated, from a particular place like a fire or the sun.

radiative zone: the inner part of the sun where energy from the center takes the form of rays.

recycle: to use things again instead of throwing them away. Recycling can help to save energy.

reflect: to throw back light, heat, or sound from a surface.

silicon: a common element.

solar cell: a device that collects sunlight and turns it into electricity.

solar furnace: a device which collects beams of sunshine. A solar furnace works like a huge magnifying glass. All the sunlight falling on a large area of lenses, or mirrors, produces a very high temperature at one small point.

solar panel: a large flat object that easily absorbs heat from the sun.

solar pond: a container filled with salt water which is used to trap the sun's heat.

solar radiation: the heat and light energy that travels through space in waves.

solar still: a container in which liquids can be separated or cleaned.

solar system: the sun and all the objects that orbit it, such as planets and moons.

star: a glowing ball of gas that gives off its own heat and light. The sun is a star.

Tokamak reactor: a special kind of chamber where atoms are fused. The name comes from the Russian words for cylinder, chamber, magnet, and coil.

tritium: a form of hydrogen. It can be made in a nuclear reactor, and is used as a fuel for nuclear fusion.

ultraviolet: rays with a shorter wavelength than the blue light we can see.

universe: all of space and everything in it.

water vapor: water as a gas.

wavelength: the distance between the top of one wave and the top of the next. It is how we measure different kinds of rays which travel in a wavy motion.

Index